215 SCIENCE C0-DVN-954
Sala, H
Harvest House   1980
0-8081-255-1

215 SCIENCE & GOD IN THE 80's
Sala, Harold
Harvest House   1980
0-8081-255-1

364

SCIENCE AND GOD IN THE 80's

Harold James Sala, Ph.D.

215/SA

HARVEST HOUSE PUBLISHERS
Irvine, California 92714

SCIENCE AND GOD IN THE 80's

Copyright © 1980 by Harvest House Publishers
Irvine, California 92714

Library of Congress Catalog Card Number 80-81473
ISBN 0-89081-255-1

Printed in the United States of America.

CONTENTS

Contents Continued

FOREWORD

The 1980's are no longer the dim, distant future—we're living in them now! The decade which confronts our world with decisions and moral choices that faced no previous generations is *today!* As a result of the scientific technology of the 1970's, we are holding in our hands more of the power of life and death than ever before.

A generation ago, only science fiction approached the possibility of deciding whether you want a male or female baby, or fathomed the possibility of a super-race cloned from a single progenitor. Unquestionably science has forced upon us moral decisions that never confronted previous generations. Yet those decisions don't have to be made in a moral vacuum, because for nearly two thousand years men and women have evaluated life in the light of God's Word, the Bible.

This book has not been written for the scientist, but for every person who wants to breach the gulf between God and science. Today the choice is not that of God *or* science; instead, it is a question of how to know God and His will in a world revolutionized by scientific advancement. Both God and science are here to stay!

Foreword Continued

The more science changes our world or gives us the possibility of shaping our own destinies, the greater the desire in most people to come to grips with the issues of life itself and to receive an answer to the question, "Where does God fit into the decisions that must be made?" Since God is changeless and eternal, no matter how our world changes in the 1980's, God will still be giving guidance and direction to those who seek it. All of us—scientists, theologians, and laymen—have needs of the heart and inner person which can be met only through a vibrant faith in God.

—Harold James Sala, Ph.D.

1

GOD AND SCIENCE

The relationship between belief in God and belief in science has been the subject of many discussions. The question is simply this: Can a person believe in God and be scientific at the same time? The answer is a sure and resounding *yes!*

German astronomer Johannes Kepler said that the scientist was an observer of God's handiwork. Said Kepler, "I give myself over to rapture. I tremble; my blood leaps. God has waited six thousand years for a looker-on to His work. His wisdom is infinite; that of which we are ignorant is contained in Him, as well as the little that we know."

Consider also Sir Isaac Newton. When the bubonic plague raged in England in 1665, Cambridge University sent all students home to await the arrest of the disease, Newton, age 23, was among these. Did he waste his time by doing nothing? Hardly. During the next 18 months he made three of the greatest discoveries in the history of human thought: the law of universal gravitation, differential and integral calculus (the basis of all modern mathematics), and the discovery of the spectrum!

Newton was once accused of having removed God from the universe and replaced His glories with mathematics. Newton was horrified. In his *Principia*, one of the greatest single feats of analysis in all of science, he wrote, "This most beautiful system . . . could only proceed from the . . . dominion of an intelligent and powerful Being."

Scientists of our day have also recognized the force of God in our universe. They have come face-to-face with questions that cannot be resolved outside God's existence.

But how about science and the Bible? When we try to harmonize the facts of God and science, we invariably meet the problem of creation. Whatever science may or may not prove about the Genesis statement "In the beginning God created the heavens and the earth," science has never proved the *absence* of God in creation.

If man by electrochemical processes succeeds in producing living protoplasm from dead substances, he will only be using his intelligence and the substances which God has given him. He will *not* prove that life on earth developed accidently. Nor will he prove that there is no God!

A lecturer told a group of boys that the proper materials beating on the ceaseless waves of a warm ocean finally resulted in a protoplasmic compound with living qualities from which more advanced forms of life ultimately emerged. The question of a 9-year-old body, "Where did the water come from?" left the speaker with a red face and no answer. Science now attempts to trace all material back to hydrogen, but we continue to ask, "Where did the hydrogen come from?" If it is now being formed, what is the source of generation? Might the ultimate answer be God?

Sir Winston Churchill asserted:

> *We rest with assurance upon* The Impregnable Rock of Holy Scripture. *Let men of science and learning expand and probe with their researches every detail of the records which have been preserved to us from the dim ages. All that they will do is to fortify the grand simplicity and*

*the essential accuracy of the recorded truths
which so far have lighted the pilgrimage of man.*

There is no conflict between the probing
analysis of science and the revelation of God. As
Sir Isaac Newton said, "The scientist is the
observer of God's handiwork." But the Bible tells
us that man may know more than the facts of
God's creation. Man may know God Himself. Do
you know Him only as a scientific fact, or do you
know Him as a Person?

2

SCIENCE AND FAITH

Dr. John McIntyre is a professor of physics and the associate director of the Cyclotron Institute at Texas A & M University. (He previously taught at Yale.) Dr. McIntyre has been recognized for his achievements in science. Writing for a current periodical, Dr. McIntyre discussed a scientist's concept of Christianity. Dr. McIntyre says:

We are sometimes told that modern minds cannot accept the 2000-year-old gospel of Jesus Christ. I first heard the gospel of Jesus Christ as a practicing physicist, and I find this opinion about the modern mind hard to understand. For when I first examined the gospel message, I found that it appealed to me in the same way that physics had first appealed to me. In fact, I concluded that my training as a physicist had given me a viewpoint and a manner of thinking that made acceptance of the gospel particularly easy.

Scientist McIntyre sees no conflict between the findings of science and the statements of the Bible. Instead, he finds that they harmonize beautifully when we remember that science deals with our world and the Bible deals with the people who inhabit the earth. The Bible is a textbook on living; science is a disciplined study of what the world is made of and the physical laws that govern it.

Dr. Charles Townes, a Nobel Prize winner from the Massachusetts Institute of Technology, is both a scientist and a Christian who is active in his church. Dr. Townes detests the thought that the Bible and science are in conflict. Says Dr. Townes:

Some accept both religion and science as dealing with quite different matters by different methods, and thus separate them so widely in their thinking that no direct confrontation is possible. To me, science and religion are both universal, and basically very similar. In fact, to make the argument clear, I should like to adopt the rather extreme point of view that their differ-

*ences are largely superficial and that the two
become almost indistinguishable if we look at the
real nature of each.*

A fellow scientist, Dean Walter, heads up the
Analytical Chemistry branch of the Metallurgy
Division of the Naval Research Laboratory in
Washington. Walter's branch investigates the
composition of metals and modern alloys. With
advanced instruments he can easily detect and
measure an impurity weighing as little as one
25-millionth of an ounce. Mr. Walter, though,
leads a double life. On weekends he finds himself
speaking in churches and civic groups about his
personal faith in God. Walter believes that a personal God is the force that holds the world
together. Scientist Walter says, "The human mind
cannot take in all that is in the world. If there is a
God, He must be bigger than all He has created.
It's rather foolish for a mind that cannot even tell
how it thinks to say, 'I think there is no God.' "

When a person thinks that science and the Bible
are in conflict, I often discover that he knows
science but not the Bible, or else the Bible but not
science. Too many times prejudice rather than investigation is the criterion of judgment. The scientist who says "I don't believe the Bible" but has
never investigated the manuscript evidence or
studied the pages of God's Word is as guilty as the

believer who condemns all the findings of science.

One last thought—there is not one God of the Bible and another God of science. There is one God, whose *Word* is revealed in the Bible and His *work* in science. Read the Bible and discover that it contains GUIDELINES FOR LIVING.

3

SCIENTISTS
WHO BELIEVE

In the not-too-distant past, some of the world's leading scientists felt that God had no place in the laboratory, and so they divorced science from faith. Louis Pasteur was typical of the breed. When asked how he could be religious and yet be a scientist, Pasteur simply replied that his laboratory was one realm and that his home and religion were a completely different realm. In all fairness, though, it must be said that for centuries the church did little to encourage scientific study. For a long time men like Galileo stood alone because he took a position contrary to the church.

In time, however, the narrow bigotism of both science and the church has given way to a realization that science and faith are not enemies at all. Actually, the scientist and the theologian are brothers in the quest for reality and truth. Long ago I came to the conclusion that the greatest disagreement is between what men say the Bible says and what it actually says. What men claim as scientific fact is often only scientific theory without the support of demonstrable facts. Many of our greatest scientists are staunch believers in God. Their faith is not a blind leap in the dark but a reasoned evaluation of the truth.

For example, there is Dr. Thomas Durant, professor of internal medicine and chairman of the Department of Internal Medicine at Temple University School of Medicine. He is also past president of the American College of Physicians. Dr. Durant says:

> We are living in the age of materialism. Anything that cannot be proven is "unscientific," and to live by faith is considered a foolish and antiquated idea. . . . We must bring the spiritual together with the scientific in medical practice. We must not be blind leaders of the blind. If we have faith in Jesus as our Saviour and Redeemer, we may then, as complete physicians, deal with the body, soul, and spirit needs of our patients.

One of our day's leading anatomists agrees. Dr. Cecil Martin is professor emeritus of anatomy at McGill University in Montreal. Dr. Martin's many years of experience lead him to conclude that "Science gives us knowledge of our physical bodies and surroundings but no insight into spiritual things. The latter can only come through the Spirit of God giving us an understanding of the revelation of Jesus Christ."

Dr. Martin continues:

> Disbelief in Christ arises, not from lack of evidence (for evidence is really conclusive), but from our spiritual unwillingness to accept the gospel. Many, therefore, ignore the gospel and try to build a substitute for it out of psychology, sociology, and political ideals, a fruitless task that ends in frustration and disappointment. But to those who take Christ at His Word, He fulfills His promise and manifests Himself in countless ways. They know Him and His power to save, and if this knowledge is not for real, then I know not what reality is.

To this statement add the words of a professor of ophthamology at the Miami School of Medicine in Florida. Dr. J. Lawton Smith says:

> For the scientist seeking to understand faith in our Lord Jesus Christ, two illustrations are furnished by radio and television. The only way the

existence of electronic waves can be detected is by their effect on a receiver. Similarly, although Jesus Christ cannot now be detected by our physical senses, His effects can be heard and seen when a man truly accepts Christ in his heart. You can prove the reality of Jesus Christ by experiment, by following His own words, "I stand at the door and knock. If any man will hear My voice and will open the door, I will come in to him and will have fellowship with him and he with me" (Revelation 3:20).

4

SCIENTIFIC METHOD

In this twentieth century the scientific method has come into its own. The tremendous advances in science which we have seen have been made as the result of dedicated research. In simplest terms, the scientific method means that a great deal of research is conducted in the area under investigation. Then, after careful analysis of the revealed facts, conclusions are reached. First facts, then conclusions.

The scientific method works in a laboratory, but can you find God through the scientific method?

Well, if you mean, "Can you measure God and
find out exactly how big He is?" The answer is no,
because that would be bringing God down to our
size—a measured, limited, finite being. God cannot be measured—He is infinite!

But if you examine the evidence of God's existence and read His revealed Word, the Bible, you
will find that it is more logical—more scientific—to
believe in God than to find alternate answers to
the evidence around us. Biologist Albert
Winchester said, "A deeper and firmer belief in
God can be the *only* result of a better insight into
truth."

Yet, strange as it may seem, sometimes those
who live by the scientific method reject God's
revelation to man without doing any research or
analysis in this field.

A college student boldly stated to me, "I have
my own religion. I am an atheist." This interested
me, so I prodded him a little further to tell me
about his religion and how his eclectic approach
had helped him. He said, "I have taken a little of
all the great religions of the world and put them
together so I have my own religion." I said, "You
must have made a thorough and exhaustive study
of the Bible. I'm sure you have studied carefully
the life of Christ and the great teachings of Scripture." He paused for a minute and said, "No, I

really haven't. In fact, I have never read the Bible."

Can you conceive of a scientist who would deny the existence of bacteria, yet who had never looked through a microscope? This is hardly scientific!

The scientific method can help you find God. After gathering evidence about God, you must take a step of faith. The Bible says, "He who comes to God must believe that He is, and that He is a rewarder of those who diligently seek Him" (Hebrews 11:6).

What is faith? It is believing what God has revealed about Himself. Saint Augustine defined faith as believing (on the basis of the Word of God) what we do not see, and its reward is to see and enjoy what we believe. In other words, if you put your faith in God, He will reveal Himself and become real to you. Accepting the existence of God is the starting point for the person who wants to find God personally.

The greatest revelation that God gave to man was His Son, Jesus Christ. "For God so loved the world that He gave His only begotten Son, that whosoever believeth in Him should not perish but have everlasting life" (John 3:16).

At one time or another you probably have met someone who had put his faith in Jesus Christ and who knew Christ in a very real way. There is no discrimination with God. As others have found Him, so can you. God will reveal Himself to you just as He did to them.

5

CREATION BY CHANCE— STATISTICALLY IMPOSSIBLE

George Gallup, the man who gained fame as a poll-taker has said, "I could prove God statistically. Take the human body alone. The chance that all the functions of the individual would just happen is a statistical monstrosity."

For a moment think with me of the intricacies of the human body. Let's start with the human brain. Ten thousand thoughts (as estimated by one scientist) pass in and out of each of our minds every day. Your brain has storage vaults that contain bits of information recorded years before. Yet the average person uses less than 10 percent of his brain!

Then there is the organ called the heart. Actually it is a muscle that contracts and forces blood through miles of veins, arteries, and capillaries. Your human body is an amazing creation. Every seven years your body is replaced with new cells that are constantly being created. As time goes on, and you grow older, this process begins to slow down, and eventually it stops.

The physical body is merely one aspect of life. How about the way the mind works? Scientists have spent years in the field of behaviorial psychology, yet these same men can't understand their wives. What about the emotions—love, hate, fear? These are complex emotions. When you stop to think about the complexities of the human body and mind, the question comes, "What is a man?" He is more than a composite of elements — he is a unique individual, unduplicated and without repetition.

Have you ever tried to think through this concept of human life? On earth are about 4½ billion people. How did they get here on this planet called earth, which hurls through space at the rate of 18.5 miles per second? Where are we headed at the end of man's physical existence? These are some of the questions that have haunted man from the beginning of time. Some people have injected the element of chance into man's appearance on this world, but when the element of chance is introduced into human life, man's appearance by chance is as likely as an unabridged dictionary's sudden appearance by chance! Creation by the act of God, or creation by chance? It is one or the other, but not both.

Suppose you believe that man was created by chance. Then you are confronted with the unanswered question, Why death? What lies beyond the grave, if anything? What is the purpose of living? There are no answers, but only gloomy pessimism, if man was created by chance. But if *God created man*, as the Bible clearly states, there is a clear answer to the question, "Where did I come from, why am I here, and what lies beyond the grave?"

6

Man Is Amazing

Nearly 3000 years ago the psalmist David wrote, "I praise Thee because I have been fearfully and wonderfully made; marvelous is Thy workmanship, as my soul is well aware" (Psalm 139:14). But just how wonderfully man really is made has come to light only in the past century, as science has begun to unlock the secrets of the human body. The human body, according to medical science, contains 30 trillion cells that reproduce themselves every seven years. Each one of the 30 trillion cells performs 10,000 different chemical functions, according to Dr. Ralph Byron of the City of Hope Cancer Clinic, yet all of them work together to produce a healthy body.

When you get tired, you can't say, "All right, cell number 26,433,293,002, get to work—you're not pulling your share of the load!" All these cells are linked together by two billion nerve cells tied into a brain containing 14 billion cells (give or take a few).

I hesitate to say that these two billion nerve cells are tied into a computer-like device called the human brain, since the human brain is far superior to any computer ever built.

A few years ago I stated that for scientists to create a computer that would duplicate the function of the human brain, you would have to produce a mechanism the dimensions of a football field and five stories high, and to cool it would require the amount of water that flows over Niagara Falls. Today miniaturization has enabled scientists to shrink the size of their computer to a mechanism weighing about three pounds, but the computer that the scientist produces is still the product of his own brain and is only as good as the information fed into it.

The marvelous human body is powered by a digestive system that contains acids strong enough to eat the varnish off a table, but which function adequately in the stomach and intestine. Apply those same acids to the backside of your hand, and they would immediately burn it, but within the human body the acids break down the foods you eat into fuel that is carried to your body through the bloodstream.

The blood is impelled by a pear-shaped muscle about the size of a man's fist. The human heart is a complex device that beats more than 2.5 million times in an average lifespan.

Recently I had breakfast with an attorney friend who serves on my board, and Wes was sporting a new cast on his arm. He had fallen while walking his dog, and he ended up with a broken arm. Adjusting to the new handicap, he reached for his mouth with his napkin, only to discover that he was closer to his ear! What a way to learn to appreciate the dexterity of your hand, which performs some 58 different movements!

And how about the marvel of the human eye, that remarkable little lens that lets you see the flowers, trees, and sunshine as it filters through the clouds? In spite of the fact that some of us find it necessary to wear glasses to correct astigmatism, our eyes continue to let us perceive the world with a third dimension that helps us walk through the forest without hitting the trees.

Glands lubricate the delicate tissues of the eye, allowing it to function year after year without burning out, as do the light bulbs of TV tubes.

"It just happened," some people say of the marvelous human body. It "just happened" about like an explosion in a printing shop producing an unabridged dictionary of the English language! Like David of old, why not pause, lift your head toward heaven, and say, "Thank you, Lord, for my health and for my body. Thank you, Father, for I am fearfully and wonderfully made."

7

ECHOES OF CREATION

Is it possible that scientists have picked up the echoes of creation? British scientist Sir Bernard Lovell believes they have. He made this astounding claim in a presidential address to the 137th annual meeting of the British Association for the Advancement of Science. Lovell, who is the director of the Jodrell Bank radio telescope, has been working with scientists at Bell Telephone Laboratories, and he reports that scientists have received radio noise 100 times stronger than could be expected. He believes that this noise, which has been picked up by extremely sensitive instruments high in the atmosphere, is nothing less than sounds of the remainder of the explosion that created the universe.

In his message, Lovell said that this recent evidence dealt a further blow to the continuous-creation theory, which has now been all but abandoned by scientists in favor of a theory which is described as the superdense-state theory of creation, or, in popular terms, the big-bang theory. Lovell believes that creation was at a definite point in time and space and that life on earth was decreed by events occurring in the first second after that explosion began. So convinced are other scientists that his findings are accurate that he could report that he is aware of "no serious criticism of his astonishing results" (using his words).

Just how do the findings of this British scientist square with the record of Scripture in the Book of Genesis? In the first three chapters of Genesis is a record of creation, given by Moses under the inspiration of the Holy Spirit. By and large, the statements of Scripture deal with the *what* of creation while much of science attempts to define the *how* of creation.

Genesis 1:1 says simply, "In the beginning God created the heavens and the earth." The word used for "create" is a Hebrew word, *bara*, which means to create from no previously existing material. It is entirely within the framework of Scripture and logic to say that the noise which Lovell thinks remains in outer space from the explosion of original creation is the result of that first creative act which Moses recorded in the passage we know as Genesis 1:1.

Sir Bernard Lovell does not state that God was the force or power behind creation—he simply says that scientists have caught faint sounds still lingering from what he calls the "primeval fireball" which gave birth to earth as we know it. It is a rather staggering thought to think that man in the afternoon of the twentieth century might be able to reach back through the centuries and record some of the noise resulting from creation in the beginning of time!

Some individuals think of science and Scripture as being enemies of each other, when actually the two deal with different aspects of the same thing. The Bible deals with *what happened*; science deals with *how it happened*. The Bible records the words of God; science records the works of God. If there is one God (which the Bible clearly teaches), then the revelation of God must be consistent. It could only follow that what God has revealed in the Bible would never be in conflict with the revelation of God in nature.

Although many scientists have failed to

recognize an eternal God as the cause behind creation, they don't all fall into that category. There
are scientists who realize the limitations of science
and also realize that the deep questions of the
human heart can ony be answered within the
framework of faith in a loving God, who brought
man into the world to have fellowship with Him.
Science, in spite of what it has done, still doesn't
tell me where I came from, why I am here, and
where I go five minutes after I die.

It is significant when science demonstrates what
the Bible says. It is amazing that Lovell's findings
should confirm what was written 3500 years ago.
But even more amazing is the fact that this great
God of creation has an interest in our lives today
in the afternoon of the twentieth century!

8

MOLECULES AND SPIRITUAL LAWS

It is almost unbelievable, but it's true—no one has ever seen a molecule. It's strange to say in our "I've-got-to-see-it-to-believe-it" world, but no one has ever seen a molecule with a naked eye. In fact, scientists have not even stopped molecules with fast cameras under high-powered microscopes! When I was in chemistry class, we used to represent molecules by colored balls held together with pieces of doweling. Scientists have never seen molecules, but they are sure they exist. They are willing to stake their lives on something they have never seen but can prove to their own satisfaction.

A molecule is the smallest bit of substance that can exist and still keep the properties of the whole substance. If you took a molecule of sugar and divided that molecule, the particles would lose the properties of sugar. Molecules are always in motion but are held together by their electrical charge. If you ask any scientist to prove the existence of molecules, he can't. But you could never convince him they don't exist, because he sees the result of their invisible existence.

How much molecules are like the existence of God! No one has ever seen God, and you can't "prove" God's existence any more than you can "prove" the existence of a molecule. But you would be just as foolish to try to *deny* God's existence as you would be to try to deny the existence of molecules. The mere existence is one of the arguments for the existence of God.

The Bible says that God is the force that holds molecules together. Nothing exists apart from its creation and sustenance by God. The Bible says not only that God is the force behind the physical laws that control our world, but also that God is the divine Architect and Creator of the world. It was He who in the beginning spoke the words and brought our world into existence.

There is another analogy that we can draw between molecules and God. Molecules are governed in their relationship to other elements by definite laws. And just as certainly we are related to God by certain spiritual laws that are as precise as the physical laws that govern the world. The Bible says that our nature creates a negative barrier between us and God, a barrier which separates us from God just as certainly as some elements are separated from other ones by their arrangement of atoms. This negative charge between us and the holy God is described in the words of Scripture as *sin*. But the Bible says that the negative charge between us and God is overcome by the influence of a third element—Jesus Christ.

When we find Christ, He imparts to us His righteousness, which in turn unites us inseparably with God. Any high-school chemistry student will vouch for the fact that when two elements meet there can be a molecular change, which in turn produces a substance entirely different from the original one. That's what Christ does in a person's life. As we trust Him as our personal Savior, our lives are united with God. The sinful nature that separates us from God is overcome by Christ, who gave His life in exchange for ours.

In simple terms, that's what the gospel is all about. Jesus Christ gave His life for you—He provided a way that we might be inseparably united with God. How about your life? Have you been united to Christ by your decision to trust Him as

Lord and Master? Becoming a Christian is not uniting with a church, but it *does* involve union with Christ. It's no chemical hocus-pocus. It is the power of God that brings salvation. Remember, there's no halfway category. Either you know Christ as your Savior, or else you are living as a stranger to God.

9

LIGHT

One of the amazing things about life is the fact that we know so little about some things which are very common, yet we take those things for granted, not sensing how important they are to our survival.

Light is a typical example. What is light? You may respond, "That's easy. Light is . . ." When you stop to think about it, a definition of light from either a practical or a scientific viewpoint isn't easy. People once thought that light was something that traveled from a person's eye to an object and then back again. If anything blocked the rays from the eye, the object could not be seen. What we know about light from a scientific viewpoint has all come in the last 300 years.

In 1666 the English scientist Sir Isaac Newton started shedding light on the nature of light when he discovered that white light is really made of many colors. About the same time a Dutch physicist contended that light consists of waves, and he proposed a wave theory to explain the behavior of light. Christian Huygens' theory held up for about a century, but then in 1864 the English physicist James Clark Maxwell proposed the mathematical theory of electromagnetism, which became the basis of modern scientific data.

But the scientific definitions aren't altogether satisfactory. For example, your lights go out and you find yourself in a very dark room. You're not satisfied with a theory—you simply want a match or a candle! That's the way many people are today. Regardless of the explanation, they simply want light in a dark world.

Simply stated, light in the world falls into three categories—natural light (sun, moon, stars, etc.), artificial light (which is another form of energy), and spiritual light. The Bible has much to say about light and what it does to darkness. The Gospel of John pictures Jesus Christ as the light of the world, who came into a world of darkness.

John says that the true light is Jesus Christ, who will give spiritual light to every person. Christ Himself said, "I am the light of the world; He who follows me shall not walk in darkness, but shall have the light of life" (John 8:12).

One of the most practical definitions of light is that it produces the cessation of darkness. Actually that definition won't hold much water scientifically, but in simple terms it does tell us something of the impact of Jesus Christ in the world. Either Jesus Christ was deceived and a deceiver, or else He brought something into this world that gives men direction and purpose for living. If you doubt the spiritual darkness in our world today, I would like to invite you to take a lingering look at our world today. Few thinking men and women would deny the fact that spiritual darkness is just as real as the darkness that shrouds planet earth on a moonless night when a storm covers the stars overhead!

10

LET THE LIGHT SHINE

For the last 3½ centuries, scientists have debated definitions of light and just what its nature is. But whether it is in the form of a laser that surgeons use in a hospital to operate on the delicate membranes of an eye, or in the form of a phosphorous match that you strike to light a candle in a backwoods shack, scientists will generally agree that light represents the release of energy, and energy represents life itself. Apart from light there would be no vegetation or even atmosphere on earth to sustain life, so in a very real sense life itself is dependent on light.

What science has discovered in the past 350 years regarding the nature of light is perfectly in accord with the statements of the world's oldest textbook on living—the Bible. Scripture tells us that God is light, and in Him is no darkness at all. It says that Christ was the true light who came into a dark world. He says, "He who follows me shall not walk in darkness, but shall have the light of life" (John 8:12). Life itself is dependent on light. This is in complete agreement with Scripture, which suggests that with the creative act of God recorded in Genesis 1 and 2, God brought not only physical life to our earth but spiritual life as well. Jesus associated darkness with sin, but light with righteousness. He said, "Men love darkness rather than light, because their deeds are evil."

He described hell as a place of outer darkness, where there is weeping and wailing. Christ spoke of His followers as men who brought light into a dark world. When Jesus told His followers, "You are the light of the world," He was in all probability within sight of the city of Safed, which was elevated above the Galilean plain. Jesus continued by saying that men do not light a candle and put it under a bushel basket, but rather on a candlestick or a candle holder so that it may give light. Then He said, "Let your light so shine before men that they may see your good works and glorify your Father in heaven" (Matthew 5:13-16).

As we move through the darkness of our day, our function as Christians should be the same as that of the lamplighter, whom Robert Louis Stevenson never forgot. One evening in his early childhood he saw a lamplighter making his rounds. So excited was the boy that he could hardly speak. He turned to his nurse and blurted out, "Look! Look! There's a man punching holes in the dark!" How can you put it better than that! Punching holes in the dark. The deepest night yields to the smallest light.

When I was a boy I visited Carlsbad Caverns—those great caves filled with intricate formations. One of the things that impressed me most was turning out the lights hundreds of feet underground, one by one, until we stood there in absolute darkness. It was so dark that to wave your hand in front of your face didn't make the slightest shadow. You could almost feel the darkness. Then the guide struck a match—only one insignificant match—but that one dim spark of fire dispelled the thick darkness and brought illumination!

"You are the light of the world" Jesus reminds His followers. Though the darkness surrounding your office or shop may be oppressive, don't run to where there is already strong light, but *be the light that drives away the gloom!* Remember, the most oppressive darkness must yield to the most insignificant light, so let the light shine!

11

THE LOWLY
PRAIRIE DOG

If you have ever been perspiring on a hot, windless day, wishing that your fan blew a little harder or your air conditioner did a little better job, let me share with you an air-conditioning system that changes the air every ten minutes and produces a breeze that is sure to cool. The credit for this system goes 100 percent to the lowly prairie dog!

These little animals, which are found on plains on every continent, build their burrows about 50 feet long and six to ten feet below the surface of the ground. This amount of space would normally provide only a five-to-ten-hour oxygen supply. To complicate the situation, the prairie dog likes company, and the more prairie dogs in the tunnel, the less oxygen there is.

How does he overcome this problem? At one end of the tunnel he builds a mound with dirt that he shovels out the end, and this mound is the real secret of his air-conditioning system. Air moving over the mound moves faster than it does over the flat end of the burrow, causing a difference in air pressure. Even the slightest breeze—as little as a half-mile per hour (it wouldn't even stir the dust)—pulls the air through the tunnel, bringing fresh oxygen and air conditioning to the prairie dog's home. And there you have another example of nature's uncanny ability to provide for its own.

But on second thought, it wasn't "nature" but God who gave that lowly animal the uncanny ability to provide for himself. When we look at a lowly little creature like the prairie dog and see his amazing ability to provide air conditioning for his burrow, we ask, "How is it possible?" Some skeptics would say that the little animal "just happened to adapt to his environment." What do you think?

In that great message called the Sermon on the Mount, Jesus called attention to the birds, indicating that the heavenly Father provides for them. Jesus said, "Look at the birds. They don't worry about what to eat; they don't need to sow or reap or store up food, for your heavenly Father feeds them." Again, Jesus said that a sparrow never falls to the earth without the heavenly Father's awareness of it.

If God is concerned with the small things of life, such as air conditioning for a prairie dog's burrow and grain that keeps sparrows alive, don't you think He is far more interested in your life and your needs? Jesus said, "The birds don't worry about what to eat; they don't need to sow or reap or store up food, for your heavenly Father feeds them." Then Jesus asked, "Are you not far more valuable to Him than they are?" Christ told us that we are to trust Him to provide for our daily needs. In the Lord's Prayer He taught us to pray, "Give us this day our daily bread. . . ." Worry has become the hallmark of life in the twentieth century, and ulcers are the badges of our faithless hearts. Put life in perspective!

12

WHY BELIEVE
THE BIBLE?

The Bible needs no defense, claim some people. It's like a lion; turn it loose and it can take care of itself. "The king of the jungle," writes my good friend Gordon Lewis, "may need no defense in his proper habitat, but he would stand little chance on a busy superhighway or in the face of modern weapons." The question is not the inherent power of the lion or the Bible. If the Bible expresses God's eternal truth, of course that needs no support from men. The question has to do with the image of the Bible in the minds of people who, for 12 to 16

years of secular education, have heard the Bible's
authority questioned and its teachings challenged.
"To defend," writes Lewis, "is to act, speak, or
write in favor of something. Do they have a right
to hear the case, if there is one, in support of the
Bible's truth?"

Some people try to avoid any confrontation.
They are quick to pounce on anyone who questions any spiritual truth. I've often concluded that
the reason they want no questions is that they
have no answers. A study of the encounters that
Jesus had with people will lead you to conclude
that Jesus never rejected the person who asked
questions in sincerity. He *did* reject the pompous
hypocrisy of the religious leaders who had answers
but the wrong ones. Christ said, "If any man is
willing to do His will, he shall know of the
teaching, whether it is of God, or whether I speak
from Myself" (John 7:17 NASB).

Why believe the Bible? Why have faith in its in-
tegrity? How would *you* answer? Without time for
elaboration, I will share with you five reasons why
I have found it much more rational to accept the
statements of Scripture about God and our world
than to deny them.

Reason Number 1—the supernatural character
of the Bible, along with its unique preservation.
Unlike most books, including most religious

writings, the Bible makes unique claims of being authored by men who wrote under the inspiration of God the Holy Spirit. Forty men over a period of 1600 years produced a document which has an organic unity and which has been uniquely preserved throughout human history. It is impossible to account for this fact by natural means. The fact of uniqueness is one of the reasons why I accept the Bible as the inspired Word of God.

Reason Number 2—the manuscript evidence supporting the claims of Scripture. Recent archeological discoveries have produced an abundance of data confirming what the Bible says. Studies of the manuscripts themselves as part of my doctoral program convinced me that the text has been conveyed without corruption from generation to generation.

Reason Number 3—the harmony of accurate secular history with biblical statements. At times the Bible has contained statements with no supporting evidence from secular history, and for that reason men denied the Bible, but later they had to eat their words because secular historical records were discovered in conformity with the statements of the Bible.

Reason Number 4—prophecy which came long before the actual event. Like what? Like Book of Daniel and its fulfillment in the Grecian period, and the many predictions about the life, death, and resurrection of Christ.

Reason Number 5—the test of pragmatism, the fact that God is alive and will meet us today as we come to Him. Some people believe that faith is a blind leap in the dark, but nothing could be farther from the truth. David Elton Trueblood put it so well when he wrote, "Faith is not belief without proof, but trust without reservation."

13

Do You
Have a Bible?

Recently I was standing in an ancient Chinese temple, now a temple of the people in Canton, China. The door to China had just begun to open to Westerners, and I was excited at the reality of getting to see China firsthand. As we listened to our guide tell how the Chinese people had been liberated from old religious beliefs, a young man who was studying English at the university approached a tourist in our group to try out his English. He spoke pleasantly for a few minutes in broad generalities, and then asked, "Do you have a Bible?"

Caught off-guard, the man replied, "Not with me, but I have one at home."

"Do you read it?" asked the young man.

Candidly the man said, "No, not much, but it's there. . . ."

Puzzled, the young Chinese man asked, "If you have a Bible, why don't you read it?"

This was no rigged political interrogation, but the searching of a young man who had been denied religious freedom all his life. He could not understand how someone could possess something so rare as a Bible and not read it.

Could I make it personal? Do you have a Bible in your home? Do you read it? Do you study it? The Bible is not a religious book which brings luck to its owner like a magic charm. Rather, it is a text-book on living, a road map that will take you by the foot of the cross to heaven's shore.

Tragic, yet true, is the fact that so many people who possess a Bible possess little understanding of this thrilling book. To me, the Bible is the record of God's dealing with man; it is like a spiritual con-tract between God and man—a valid agreement of what God will do if man follows the stipulations of the agreement.

The Bible tells us that, even as there are physical laws that govern the universe, there are also spiri-tual laws that govern our relationship with God. It tells a person how to become a Christian, how to learn to pray so that his prayers are answered, how to live a life that is above the carnal tug of sensual lust, and how to find peace of mind and the assurance that his sins are forgiven.

The tourist who was approached by the Chinese youth possessed a Bible, but the Bible and its leading Personality—Jesus Christ—had never possessed him. Owning a Bible only points the way; it doesn't guarantee your entrance into heaven. True, it tells you how to become a Christian, but it isn't a passport that guarantees arrival at the end of the trip. Do you read your Bible? Maybe you don't read it because it doesn't make sense to you. If that's the case, I suggest that you begin by meeting its Author, for only then will His book make sense to you.

Scores of men and women have told me personally, "Once I received Jesus as my personal Savior, the Bible became alive and I understood it." "The natural man," wrote the Apostle Paul, "receives not the things of the Spirit of God, for they are foolishness to him; neither can he know them, because they are spiritually discerned" (1 Corinthians 2:14). Don't just possess a Bible; let it possess you!

THE BIBLE AND
THE 1980'S

We were flying at an altitude of about 40,000
feet. I had just picked up a book and started
reading it when I noticed that the bearded youth
beside me was reading along with me. He had read
the Oriental mystics, the philosophers of the ancient Middle East, and even a few college texts, but
he had never seen anything quite like the book I
was reading. His interest in my book amused me,
but I said nothing and kept reading.

Finally he could stand it no longer and said,
"What is that book you are reading?" I replied, "It

is a commentary on the last book of the New Testament—the Book of Revelation. Revelation is almost 2000 years old, but it is as relevant as your newspapers. In it God tells us about the future and what is going to happen. It's like history pre-recorded."

For centuries the Bible has been a trustworthy record of God meeting the needs of men and women. It is as contemporary as guilt, hate, frustration, atomic energy, space travel, and heart transplants. The question that is in the minds of many people is this: "How do I know that the Bible isn't just another book?"

The Bible endures the passing of the centuries as no other book ever written. Scholars all over the world have in their possession ony 13 manuscripts of Plato, the great Greek philosopher. We possess only one manuscript of the annals of Tacitus, the Roman historian who lived during the second century. We have only a few manuscripts of Sophocles, Euripides, Vergil, and Cicero, yet there are more than 13,000 manuscripts in existence containing all or part of the Bible! There are more than 4000 ancient Greek manuscripts, 8000 Latin manuscripts, and another 1000 ancient versions, making a grand total of more than 13,000 ancient manuscripts for scholars to study.

On many occasions men have decided to

destroy the Bible once and for all. King Jehoiakim tried to burn the manuscripts. In 303 A.D. the Roman emperor Diocletian ordered every Bible in the Roman empire to be burned, but ten years later he died, and his successor, Constantine, made Christianity the faith of the empire. In the Middle Ages the institutional church attempted to keep the Bible from the common man. Agnostics and infidels railed against it, but still it stands.

The French atheist Voltaire said, "Christianity shall not survive me by one hundred years." Yet after his death the British Bible Society bought his home in Geneva and printed an entire edition of the Bible on his press! One hundred years after Voltaire's death, the British government purchased Codex Sinaiticus, a New Testament manuscript dating to 350 A.D., for the sum of $500,000 from the Russian government. But that same year a first edition of Voltaire sold for only 11 cents!

Space doesn't allow a description of the highly important manuscripts of the ancient Scriptures that have been found in Jordan and Israel since 1957 in and around Qumran—manuscripts that were placed there when the Roman army marched against Israel in about 70 A.D. Some of those manuscripts of the Old Testament that were previously in the possession of scholars. Are these things coincidence? No other book ever written makes the claim that it will endure forever, but the Bible does. It says, "The Word of the Lord endures forever" (1 Peter 1:25).

15

GENETIC ENGINEERING

Genetic engineering is a new term to describe what happens when DNA molecules are split by enzymes and recombined with other substances. With the exception of splitting the atom (first accomplished by Enrico Fermi and his colleagues at the University of Chicago), no other feat has so divided scientific opinion.

When *Time* magazine did a cover story on genetic engineering, they captioned their lead article "Tinkering With Life." The *New York Times* likewise expressed concern as they titled a recent article on the subject "New Strains of Life or Death." Their subtitle says, "Scientists have learned to rearrange the basic genetic material of living things, and so have opened an exciting new research frontier, but one biologist warns, 'the future will curse us for it.'"

At a recent U.S. Senate hearing on the dangers of genetic engineering, Representative Matthew Rinaldo said that DNA research is potentially more dangerous than nuclear bombs. Joseph Califano, the Secretary of Health, Education and Welfare, asked Congress to impose federal restrictions on recombinant DNA and E coli bacteria until it has been demonstrated that the result is not a monster that could destroy the human race.

A number of major scientists are likewise concerned. George Wald, a Nobel laureate, supports efforts to ban DNA research, contending that science would be better off spending its time fighting disease by purifying the environment. The City Council of Cambridge, Massachusetts (where Harvard University is located) was so disturbed over DNA research that they passed a law banning research until a citizens' panel was convinced of its safety.

The U.S. National Institute of Health has gotten into the picture too, laying down guidelines for doing DNA research, but so far their efforts have been rather feeble.

What's the big furor over? Why is there such apparent concern over DNA? Is it merely a scare such as has accompanied scientific breakthrough down through the centuries, or is there real cause for concern?

When DNA molecules are recombined with other substances, a new enzyme is produced which has the capability of reproducing itself at a very rapid rate. The *New York Times* explains the situation by saying that it is feared that "the biologists who propose to tamper with the apparatus of micro-organisms would create a new Andromeda-like strain that might escape their control and spread an incurable disease to the population."

The chairman of the department of biology at prestigious Cal Tech fears the shattering of what he calls nature's "evolutionary barrier" between different kinds of creatures—the genetic incompatibility that in most cases prevents one specie from breeding with another.

Other scientists are convinced that DNA recombinants are perfectly harmless. Bernard Davis, a Harvard Medical School microbiologist, is so sure that the new life is safe that he has offered to drink recombinant DNA. But Cal Tech's Robert Sinsheimer counters, "Biologists have become, without wanting it, the custodians of great and terrible power. It is idle to pretend otherwise."

16

DNA—
Right or Wrong?

In the film "Demon Seed," a scientist's wife is assaulted by a supersmart computer which manages to combine its genes with hers, and the resultant offspring is a kind of invincible superman.

A few years ago most people would have written off such a plot as science-fiction nonsense, but genetic engineering involving the rearrangement of genes has now made such bizarre events a near-possibility. *Time* magazine's cover story entitled "Tinkering with Life" explains:

About five years ago, California scientists learned how to combine genes from different organisms regardless of how low or high they are on the evolutionary scale. Though the researches added only one or two new genes, the creation of such hybrid molecules was a stunning fear.

There are two major concerns revolving around DNA recombinant research. One is the fear that a super-Andromeda-type bacteria will escape the laboratory, which could wipe out the human race. That fear has some foundation, since the new DNA substances become a virile laboratory of rapidly producing enzymes. The second fear is that, by recombining genes, scientists may be able to produce a master race of hybrid creatures, such as would result by crossing a gorilla and a human.

What are the moral and spiritual implications of DNA research? That's the question confronting thoughtful scientists. The first concern—that DNA research may produce a monster-type bacteria—is a real threat. Prior to the splitting of the atom in 1945, some religious leaders said that it would never be done—that God would not allow man to tamper with the basic nuclear structure of the universe. But Enrico Fermi and his colleagues at the University of Chicago did it, and when the first A-bomb was dropped, 70,000 people immediately died and another 66,000 were injured. As Caryl Rivers put it, "Some nightmares turn solid. . . . The human capacity to destroy can outrun even the human imagination."

What about the second fear? In the Book of Genesis, God made it clear that both man and animals were to reproduce after their kind. The Old Testament Law clearly forbad sexual relations between humans and lower forms of life; therefore, it could only follow that genetic research crossing the genes of two species would never have the blessing of God. As a Ph.D. in Bible who has followed with keen interest some of the DNA accomplishments, I believe that God has placed certain barriers or limits to the accomplishments of the probing mind of science, and that man, regardless of his efforts, will not cross them. God clearly told Jonah that he has set barriers or limits on the earth and that man cannot cross them. Just where they are remains to be seen.

In a real sense, DNA recombinants are amoral; it is *how they are used* that will determine whether they are right or wrong. Through gene surgery, DNA research offers the hope of curing cancer and of eliminating diseases which are inherited, such as diabetes and hemophilia. Such research offers a host of inexpensive new vaccines and related benefits which would serve mankind with blessing. Like the two-edged sword, it remains to be seen whether DNA recombinants will bless us or curse us.

17

TEST-TUBE BABIES

The New Biology of the late 1970's has forced upon the world unprecedented moral and ethical questions. DNA recombinant enzymes make it possible for genes of different species (as apes and man) to be matched, which conceivably could lead to the crossing of specie lines.

New Biology has already produced life in a test tube. In 1950 Dr. Landrum Shettles of Columbia University announced that he had achieved fertilization of a human ovum in a test tube and had maintained the human embryo's life for six days.

Then in 1959 an Italian scientist, Dr. Daniele Petrucci, working at the University of Bologna, claimed that he had fertilized an ovum *in vitro* (in glass), and that the human embryo had lived for 59 days, although it had become enlarged and deformed. Pope John XXIII roundly condemned the scientist. As the result of the moral outcry that was raised, Petrucci discontinued his research, but other scientists haven't been dissuaded, and have made considerable progress toward producing an artificial womb capable of producing human life in a laboratory.

Another aspect of the test-tube controversy is the implanting of a human embryo in a woman's body, which would then bring the fetus to full maturity. In other words, one woman's body could be used to produce another woman's child.

What right does science have to delve into manipulating human embryos? What are the moral implications? Paul Ramsey, the Yale theologian who has written extensively on the ethics of genetic control, is an outspoken critic of genetic manipulation, including test-tube fertilization. Speaking as one voice, both Protestants and Catholics have criticized embryonic manipulation.

Pope John made the position of the Roman Catholic Church clear when he condemned Daniel Petrucci's experiment. Unquestionably, the Bible makes it clear that God's plan is for children to born of the union of a husband and wife. It centers in an age-old institution—the home—and apart from God's plan He makes no provision for human birth.

Harold Green, professor of law at George Washington University, said, "I think it's time now for society to ask itself whether we want to go through the door of this brave new world. It's time to start thinking about these elements while research is still underway, or even before it gets underway." Author Caryl Rivers raises the legal implications of what would happen when a damaged child results from an embryo transplant. Can the parents or donor sue the doctor for malpractice?

How far does God's patience go with scientists who play God? It is little wonder that when psychiatrist Johannes Burgers retired from the University of Maryland, he was so alarmed about genetic experimentation and manipulation that he proposed a 50-year moratorium on work of this nature. He said, "It may sound antiprogressive. I would not want to make it forever. But for the moment, wait. Wait until you know more about life."

18

Mail-Order Offspring

You want a child, so the doctor asks you to fill out a form indicating whether you want a boy or a girl, a child with blue eyes or brown, taller than you or about the same, interested in electronics or in poetry. Absurd? It is today, but it may not be in the future if genetic engineering continues its astonishing progress. Genetic engineering has already sparked more controversy than any advancement of science since the birth of the nuclear age, in the early 1940's.

Scientists, lawmakers, and citizens' groups are

hotly debating man's newfound power to manipulate genetic material. Genes are like a set of blueprints that determine all the characteristics of an organism, and eventually of a life. Nothing is more fundamental to life and heredity than genes, for they determine the characteristics of life, including the physiognomy of a person—whether he has blue or brown eyes, whether he is tall or short, whether he has a long nose or a short nose, whether he has pretty teeth or could eat corn on a cob through a tennis racket. Your genes were passed on to you from your parents.

Scientists have in their grasp the ability to split genes and to drastically alter the future of humanity. They are coming close to the point where they can play God by manipulating life itself. The ramifications are tremendous.

Genetic engineering became a reality in 1973, when scientists discovered that genetic materials could be chopped up and then recombined, putting the materials together in such a way that a new set of genes is produced—hence the new term "gene splicing." This in itself isn't necessarily evil. For example, this technique is now used in the making of insulin (which previously was taken from the pancreas of sheep or oxen). Through gene splicing scientists have discovered a bacterium which will produce insulin in vast quantities—which is a much better way of producing the substance than extracting it from sheep or oxen. But what happens if a substance is produced in the laboratory which escapes and infects or kills thousands of people?

This sounds like something which a movie scriptwriter dreamed up, but it isn't. What I have just described could actually happen, and this is one of the reasons for the great concern. Only months ago scientists were told that through clever tricks a genetic engineer had succeeded in producing and inserting into common bacteria a substance that gives instructions for producing an important human brain hormone. If that substance ever got out of control, tremendous human suffering would result.

As Professor Paul Schimmel of the Massachusetts Institute of Technology put it:

> Genetic engineering is an extraordinary achievement of science and technology. The potential benefits are immense, but there are enough dangers and unknowns that it could become a curse instead of a blessing. Which it will be depends upon the conscientious participation of all of us in the decisions that govern this activity. Christians must maintain a spiritual perspective and encourage that perspective

among others. In these ways, we can assure that our scientific explorations into genetics bring the blessings they're intended to give.

It's something to think about!

19

CLONING

Adolph Hitler set out to produce a master race by destroying cultures and races which he considered to be inferior to Aryan forebears. Today scientists have made it possible to produce a master race through genetic manipulation—which is wracked with controversy. Cloning (as the process has come to be known) is such a new word that it isn't found in many contemporary dictionaries, and when it is found in dictionaries, it is used in reference to animals and plants but not in reference to human reproduction.

Here's how it began.

In 1968, J.B. Gurdon of Oxford University produced a frog by taking an unfertilized egg cell from an African clawed frog and then destroying its nucleus by ultraviolet radiation. He then replaced this nucleus with the nucleus of a cell of *another* frog of the same specie. The egg, suddenly finding itself with a full set of chromosomes, began reproducing. The result was a tadpole that was a perfect twin of the frog that had donated the cell. If this were done at the human level, an individual could reproduce himself perfectly and completely in another person. In other words, a man would be the identical twin of another person without fathering the child.

Scary? You bet it is. The basic rights of an individual to have a family could be destroyed. Under the guise of the betterment of humanity, individuals could be denied the right of reproduction. Cities or even nations of individuals who are identical in appearance could emerge.

Cloning means that one person could produce a child with the genetic cells of a donor. The system isn't entirely foolproof, however. Scientists are still looking for what they call the "switch on." Whatever it is that causes the cells of the donor to begin reproducing isn't entirely clear, but scientists think they've almost discovered it.

In March 1978, scientists announced a major

step toward finding the substance that switches on the reproduction of cells. Ann Brothers of the University of Indiana and her colleagues believe that they are only one step away from being able to put it all together. Test-tube fertilization, which has now been accomplished (along with DNA recombinant enzymes), are steps toward the completion of the process.

Will it ever actually happen? Some people are convinced that God alone holds the master switch, and they may well be right. But even if DNA recombination is accomplished, this shouldn't rock your faith. What most people fail to realize is that, unlike God in His creative acts, scientists are working with *already created* substances which respond in a definite way to stimuli according to the natural laws which are controlled by God.

Who put the physical laws controlling our universe into effect? Who said that two atoms of hydrogen and one atom of oxygen will always produce an atom of water? Scientists are still working within a system of orderly process.

Nevertheless, science is rapidly moving into an area that would put it against the time-honored institution of marriage and family relations. It is quite predictable that most segments of society shrink back in fear at the thought of scientific processes that could create a master race of individuals and at the same time restrict other individuals from participating in the parenting process. Lest science turn into a Frankenstein, we have no alternative but to police the laboratory, so that our genius doesn't become a monster and destroy us.

20

MORAL IMPLICATIONS OF THE NEW BIOLOGY

Has science become its own enemy? There are indications that science and technology are moving in a direction that could result in their own demise. In the last decade, a new list of related terms has come into our vocabulary. Genetic engineering, new biology, cloning, *in vitro* conception, cryogenics, and other terms all relate to research which has created as much dissent as anything in our generation.

Most of these terms revolve around DNA research, which according to scientists is the very key to life itself. The thrust of science in this area means that people are now being confronted with situations which God never intended us to face. If a moratorium on genetic research is not declared soon, or at least clear guidelines imposed on an international level, scientists will confront us with even more bizarre situations.

The New Biology could alter the parenting process. It could threaten the very right to life, which is a God-given determinant. Science must be our servant—not our master. The fundamental right of an individual to reproduce after his kind must not be lost, or else Adolph Hitler's mythical master race will have been ushered in on the gleaming wings of science. If science threatens the basic rights of an individual, the very goal of science has been lost and a repressive mantle has been thrown on mankind. The New Biology demands a study of morality and ethics clothed in the clearly defined will of God.

Where does man find answers to questions of ethics and morality if not in the pages of God's Word, the Bible? Traditionally, science and faith have not been very good bedfellows. Scientists have denounced theologians as obscurantists and have called them old-fashioned. At the same time, the church has often opposed scientific research and condemned those who indulge in it. But actually, theology and science should be two disciplines of the same substance.

There is one God who has revealed His Word in Scripture and His work in science. If the thrust of science were cross-referenced by the moral and spiritual implications of Scripture, we would not be facing the moral dilemmas of New Biology. On the other hand, if the dogmas of the church were cross-referenced by the actual facts of science, a lot of scientists would not feel that it is a matter of following Christ and forsaking science, or vice versa.

Because science has not been concerned with moral and spiritual issues, we are now confronted with a growing possibility that some of the recent scientific accomplishments will bring the condemnation of Christians everywhere. The issue at stake is not science—it is *the unethical and immoral use of science and technology*. Fire that bakes the bread and warms the body can also burn down the house! Splitting the atom has resulted in medical technology that has saved thousands of lives, but when used unscrupulously the same technology could result in bringing devastation to large segments of the human race. DNA recombinant enzymes may turn out to be a benefactor of humanity, but when used unscrupulously they could produce a curse of unprecedented proportions.

21

Growing
Nuclear Stockpiles

World nuclear stockpiles, according to the Stockholm International Peace Research Institute, amount to about 50,000 megatons. A megaton is the equivalent of one million tons of TNT. With the world's population now standing at about 4.5 billion people, this means that for every man, woman, boy, and girl on the face of our earth there is the equivalent of 15 tons of TNT stockpiled somewhere ready to be used in a nuclear holocaust!

In the years since Hiroshima and Nagasaki,

more than 10,000 tactical nuclear weapons have been stockpiled, which are the equivalent of 700 million tons of TNT, or about 50,000 Hiroshimas! The Stockholm Institute estimates that the nations of the world have spent more than seven trillion dollars on armaments since the conclusion of World War Two.

There aren't enough zeros on your calculator to tell you how much money that represents for every person today, but the greatest enemy is not the one across the ocean—it is the one within ourselves. History proves conclusively that there has never been a major arms buildup which didn't eventually result in warfare. It is fragile comfort to know that more people may die "over there" than over here!

In the early 1960's I brought a commentary on thermonuclear warfare and quoted Major General Robert Taylor, whose words bear repeating. As true as they were then, they are even more pungent today:

> Our world today needs men who can think straight about life's values, about human relationships, and about divine design. Moral stability, integrity of character, and meaningful living . . . have a basis in spiritual resources.
> What would happen if the 400,000 scientists who are at work in our world developing and im-

proving weapons of warfare could turn loose their creative energies and attack the problem of hunger, of literacy, and of disease? Just what potential for mankind could result if man could beat his sword into a plowshare, and his spear into a pruning-hook? Dreamer! Do-gooder! Philologizer! Perhaps! Because the blunt facts of reality are that what I would like to see will not happen. Jesus said, "There shall be wars and rumors of wars, but the end is not yet. . . ."

How does a person react to the news that there is the equivalent of 15 tons of TNT for every person on earth? Does this cause you to wonder just what kind of world your children will grow up in? For the Christian there is a strange irony. Christ said that our reaction is not to be fear or distress. Rather, it is to be that of joy, for we know that the only real security lies in Jesus Christ. He said, "When you see these things come to pass, lift up your heads, for your redemption draws near."

Before he died, Arnold Toynbee, the British historian and foe of nuclear armament, said, "There is no turning back today." He meant that the shadow of a nuclear umbrella has descended over the globe, and that there is no turning back the calendar. We've got to learn to live with it —no, live above it—setting our affections on things above, which cannot be destroyed by chain reactions and nuclear fission.

22

How Do You Know There Is a God?

The young Communist student looked his guest in the eye as he said, "Do you mind if I ask you three questions? First—how can you be so sure there is a God? Can you prove God's existence? Second—how do you know that the Bible is true? Third—if there is a God, why does He allow so many people to suffer?

If you were confronted with those three questions and had one minute to answer each, what would you say? I would be tempted to point out that apart from God—not just any god, but the revealed God of the Bible—there is an emptiness in the heart of man that can never be filled.

The French philosopher Blaise Pascal wrote of the vacuum in the heart of every man which can be filled only by Jesus Christ. Having traveled in Communist countries, and having had contact with people who have grown up in those same countries, I am convinced that there is an emptiness in the hearts of men and women, and that the three questions asked by the 17-year-old honor student are three questions without answers in the writings of Marx and Lenin.

I would like to tell our friend about the letter which came recently to our Cambodian associate who translates and broadcasts my radio program, *Guidelines*, to Cambodia. This was a letter from a Communist soldier who wrote the following: "I listen to your programs every day, morning and evening. . . . I would like to be a Christian like you too. How can I become a Christian like you? Please help me."

But merely pointing out the fact that Communism doesn't answer those questions doesn't tell what Christianity's answer is, either. Attacking the deficiency of one system doesn't prove the superiority of the other. How can you prove God's existence? Were the Russian cosmonauts right who went into space saying they looked for God but didn't see Him in outer space? The Bible accepts God's existence and tells us about His involvement in the affairs of men. I can give you some logical reasons for accepting God's existence—reasons that have spoken to the hearts of men for centuries: the cause-and-effect relationship of our world; the design which demands a Designer; the moral sense of oughtness which causes men to worship a Creator.

I can't "prove" God's existence, but I can demonstrate how much more logical it is to accept His existence than to reject Him. I would like to point out the fact that God is not a philosophical abstraction, as many religions teach, but is a personal being who has revealed Himself to mankind. In striving to understand all there is to know about God before even believing in Him, some people fail to grasp the central fact of His existence and the truth of His revelation to us in the Person of Jesus Christ.

The irony of my answer is even though I can't "prove" God's existence to you, I can introduce you to Him by letting you meet His Son, Jesus Christ, who lived, died, and proved His deity by rising from the dead. Unlike other religious leaders, Jesus Christ challenged men to put His teaching and truth to the test. "If any man is willing to know of the teaching," challenged Jesus, "whether it be of man or of God, he shall know it." If Jesus did rise from the dead, authenticating the very heart of the New Testament, He demands not only my worship and acknowledgment, but also my life and existence.

23

WHERE IS GOD?

Where is God's heaven? Robert Jastrow thinks he may know. Jastrow is one of the world's best-known scientists, having outstanding credentials. He has served as professor at Dartmouth and Columbia Universities and has been actively involved in the U.S. space program. He is also the author of a disturbing book entitled *Until the Sun Dies*.

Dr. Jastrow says that the evidence for God is all around us, and that current theories about the nature of the universe point to His existence, but that most scientists don't like the notion of God's existence and are distressed when they are confronted with it, even though the evidence cannot be denied or avoided. He says that the evidence for creation points to a single creative act taking place by a force of unimaginable power. And here's why he believes this.

Scientists know that galaxies are moving away from us at a tremendous rate of speed. The farther out they are, the faster they go, even pushing the speed of light. The only explanation, Jastrow believes, is a gigantic explosion which he believes was caused by God. In his book he says that most scientists contend for a closed universe. In other words, they believe that there is an endless recreation, and that creation is merely part of the cycle which never ends.

Jastrow doesn't believe that. He says that God has to be the force that started the whole ball of earth spinning. If enough mass were out in space, then it is conceivable that the continuous theory of creation might be plausible, but, according to Jastrow, there just isn't enough mass out there. "Rather than grapple with the implications," he says, "they try to ignore it." Continuing, the scientist says, "it is an interesting psychological fact . . . in effect, we have proven the existence of God if you don't watch your language. A layman would put it that way, and I like to put it that way because it's humbling. It exposes certain weaknesses in the structure. And out of those weaknesses, as was always the case, come great new advances."

Robert Jastrow, a man with a brilliant academic background, is saying an old thing in a new way. David, the shepherd boy and amateur astronomer of Israel, said it 3000 years ago: "The heavens declare the glory of God and the firmament shows His handiwork." The further we probe into space, the more data are revealed which point to the creative act of God mentioned by Moses in the Book of Genesis.

24

Is Immortality Real?

When the late Senator Everett Dirksen was asked the question found in the Book of Job, "If a man die, shall he live again?" Dirksen replied, "Surely he shall, as surely as the day follows night, as surely as the stars follow their courses, as surely as the crest of every wave brings its trough." Dirksen stands in good company when he says that death is the beginning and not the end, for the greatest men throughout the centuries—both believers and nonbelievers—have contended for life after death.

Socrates, Plato, Kant, Goethe, physicist Arthur Compton, Albert Schweitzer, Henry James, Thomas Edison, Blaise Pascal, and a host of others have contended for the immortality of the soul. I personally like the way the Indian philosopher and poet Rabindranath Tagore put it: "Death is not extinguishing the light; it is putting out the lamp because the dawn has come."

The man who really brought the electric light bulb to the world was a pragmatic, hard-working inventor by the name of Thomas Edison. I have no way of knowing if Edison ever heard Tagore's comment, but I know he would have agreed. When Edison lay dying, his doctor leaned over to hear him whisper, "It is very beautiful over there." And soon Edison was gone.

The skeptic may say, "Yes, that's well and good, but what you have shared is basically what men have said about eternal life—their beliefs or comments," and the skeptic is right. Most of the comments about immortality are made by men on this side of death, and they base their arguments on logic instead of on observation. But if someone had actually been there—had crossed the threshold of death and come back to give us an authoritative report of what it is—then it would be easier to accept as fact, thinks the skeptic. Well, what about the research of thanatologist Elizabeth Kubler-Ross? Isn't that what she has done? Not really, since most her work centers around people who have been declared "clinically dead" but were revived to give us their impressions of life after death.

But if someone had been dead for *several days* and then came back, would that make a difference? There is such a Person. His name is Jesus Christ, and He is alive today. For 33 years He lived among us, and then He was crucified at the hands of the Romans. For three days He was dead— as dead as professional executioners can make a man. Then, says the well-attested record of history, He came forth from the grave. He said, "I am the resurrection and the life. He who believes in me, though he were dead, yet shall he live, and he who lives and believes in me shall never die."

If Jesus did rise from the grave, as both secular history and the church of Jesus Christ contend, then what Christ taught about immortality becomes valid and authoritative, no matter how it may differ from other religious documents that talk about immortality. The difference is that Jesus was truly dead but actually came back from the grave. This renders His words authoritative. He has been there and has conquered our old enemy, death. "Because I live," said Jesus, "You shall live also." Do you have that assurance? You can find it in the pages of Christ's biography in the New Testament. Read it today!

25

DOES GOD HAVE A SENSE OF HUMOR?

"Does God really lack a sense of humor?" That question was the lead sentence in an article by a *Times* magazine religion writer, John Dart. I read the article and was ready to discard it, but then I set it aside and started thinking about it. John Dart's provocative article asked a question but really didn't give the answer, so I began some research of my own.

On the negative side of the ledger, if you look up the three passages in Scripture where it is said that God laughs, you find that He laughs at the foolishness of the wicked rather than with the righteous who are having a chuckle over something funny. But does that mean that God has no sense of humor?

If tradition counts, you have to put God's humor on the negative side of the ledger, because the church has generally followed the attitude of St. John Chrysostom, who lived about the fourth century. Chrysostom said, "Laughter does not seem to be a sin, but it leads to sin." Thus Christians have often associated God with black clerical garbs and long faces.

That fact was born out by an incident that took place in England as a huckster was going from door to door collecting trash and particularly old glass bottles. Knocking on the door of a certain woman known to be a rather dour Christian, he asked, "Got any old whiskey bottles, lady?"

Furrowing her brow, she replied, "Do I look like I would drink whiskey?"

"Okay, lady, then vinegar bottles?"

On the positive side of the ledger, it is evident that Jesus, in spite of the seriousness of His life and His mission, had a sense of humor. The humor of Christ is often robed in innuendoes which are lost in translation. When He told His disciples, "Go tell that old fox Herod . . ." this must have brought a smile to their faces! The Quaker scholar Elton Trueblood in his book *The Humor of Christ* contends that the humor of our Lord is readily apparent when searched out and is most clearly shown through the irony and paradox in His exchanges with people.

Though there is no clear reference to any occasion when Jesus laughed, I am confident that He did laugh and could see humor in the ironies of life. One of the reasons that humor has a place in the Christian's life is that humor is directly related to Christian virtues. If a man is at peace with himself, it is easy to smile or laugh at himself, but when he is uptight and angry with himself and the world, he is more apt to strike at himself than to laugh at himself.

Christian humorist Mary Betten Mitchell sees humor related to humility, and believes that the proud person can't laugh at himself because it just hurts too much. Says Mrs. Mitchell, "People can laugh at their embarrassing moments after weeks or months, but can they do it at the end of the same day? The really advanced humorist-Christian finds something funny about a frustrating situation right away. That requires a certain amount of humility."

26

WHY DOES GOD
ALLOW SOME THINGS?

That old question, "Why, God? Why do you allow some things?" is as old as humanity itself. From the earliest days, people have been trying to reconcile the basic goodness of God with some of the calamities that happen to us.

Many sincere, trusting individuals pondered the answer to that question when Paul Little dies as the result of injuries sustained in an automobile accident. Little, age 47, was the director of Inter-Varsity Christian Fellowship, a student organization with a worldwide impact.

Little's activities weren't confined to the student world, however. His personality and charm endeared him to people of all age groups, and without question it could be said of Little that he was one of the outstanding Christian leaders of his day. When Little died, more than one individual asked himself why God in His sovereign wisdom would allow that to happen with this life that was making such a great impact on a segment of society often overlooked. Yet perhaps that very question contains the answer itself—that God is sovereign, and that His ways and wisdom are above human understanding.

Only weeks before his death, Little wrote in *Decision* magazine that often the supreme test of faith for the Christian relates to the question "whether or not God is good." He said, "In the face of tragedy, only trust in His character will carry us through." Paul Little's death reminded me of the fact that very often it is hard for us to fully understand the plan of the Father.

I was reminded of the death of Dawson Trotman, founder of the Navigators—an organization which emphasizes the study of God's Word and which has touched millions of lives. When Trotman drowned, men and women asked the same question: "Why?"

The list of those whose lives were cut short in-

cludes such men as Willis Shank, missionary pilot
and Christian statesman, whose plane went down
in the Artic, and Dr. Paul Carlson, medical doctor
who gave his life in the Congo rebellion. And
what of Nate Saint, Jim Elliot, and their compan-
ions, who died on the sandy landing strip of a river
in Ecuador? Many more names could be added of
people who gave their lives in the service of Christ
or whose lives were cut short by accident or injury.

Each of these people endorsed the words of Paul,
who wrote to the Philippians that his desire
was that Christ should be glorified in his body,
whether by life or by death. God can use the un-
timely death of one of His servants to speak to the
hearts of many others, who will step out from the
ranks to follow in the path of Christian service.
Following Nate Saint's death, his sister Rachel carried on the work with the Aucas, and now the
Aucas themselves are sending missionaries to
other tribesmen.

The third thing which must be said is that our
faith in Christ does not make us immune to
natural disasters, even though it gives us the
assurance that death opens the door to eternal life.
Paul wrote to the Corinthians, "To be absent from
the body is to be present with the Lord" (2 Corinthians 5:8). Later he wrote, "For me to live is
Christ and to die is gain" (Philippians 1:21)

27

How Big Is God?

How big is God? Ask ten people, and you'll get ten different answers. Ask a South American Indian deep in the jungles of Columbia and he may lead you to a primitive hut. From a narrow shelf just under a hand-thatched roof he may take down a beautifully polished statue and hold it out, saying, "God is this big. . . ." As you observe the statue he holds in his hand, you notice that it bears a striking resemblance to the man who holds it!

Ask a stockbroker in Tokyo or Manila, "How

big is God?" and he might say, "That all depends."
You ask, "On what?" He answers, "It depends on
the stock market, or your bank account, or the
scope of your influence. . . ." He carefully avoids
your question, but you sense that he is really saying, "Materialism has really become my god, for all
that counts to me is what I can get my hands on."
He's not interested in anything he can't see or
bank or declare as an asset.

If you went to a college campus and asked a professor, "How big is God?" he might smile accom-
modatingly and say, "Those of us in education
today don't think of God in concrete terms. We
think of God in terms of the expanding fields of
knowledge and scientific research. God made the
intellect, and we believe that the manifestation of
wisdom and knowledge is what really counts. We
can't buy this medieval nonsense connected with
how many angels can stand on the head of a pin."

Suppose you stop a sophomore college student
and ask him that question, "How big is God?" He
might say, "Is that a question I'll have on a test?"
But then, getting serious, he might say, "God—I
don't think about God, and I won't until I'm old.
Right now I'm living it up—wine, women, and
song. Who knows how long we've got till some
politician pushes the button and blows us all up?
Now is my time for fun!" But the question still remains, "How big is God?"

One of the oldest of all historical dramas took place in the Book of Job, in your Bible. About the time of Abraham, or possibly before, Job looked up toward heaven and asked himself the same question. Then he said, "Can you by searching find out God? Can you find out the Almighty unto perfection? It is as high as heaven; what can you do? Deeper than hell; what can you know? The measurement thereof is longer than the earth and broader than the sea" (Job 11:7-9). Job would say "No, God is bigger than anything that can be measured." No wonder the Psalmist declared, "Great is the Lord and greatly to be praised. His greatness is unsearchable" (Psalm 145:3)!

How big is God? He is bigger than your financial need. How big is God? He is greater than the need of your life—greater than the problems that confront your business, your home, and your marriage. Bigger than the energy crisis, bigger than the conflict that divides individuals and groups and even nations.

How big is God? He is bigger than the greatest need of your heart.

God says, "Come now, let us reason together, saith the Lord; though your sins be as scarlet, they shall be as white as snow; though they be red like crimson, they shall be as wool" (Isaiah 1:18).

God is greater than your wildest imagination, but He is limited by one thing—your refusal to let

Him work in your life. He invites you to come to Him, but He never forces His will upon you. Jesus said, "Come to me, all you who labor and are heavily burdened, and I will give you rest. . . ." (Matthew 11:28). It's His invitation to you to discover His true greatness!

If you would like additional help or counsel, or would like to know more about personally receiving Jesus Christ as your Savior, write to Dr. Sala at the address closest to you.

In the United States write to:

Dr. Harold Sala
Box G
Laguna Hills, CA 92653

In Asia write to:

Dr. Harold Sala
Box 2041
Manila, Philippines